D0773551

MVFOL

Baby-sitting Smarts

Jil Fine

HIGH
interest
books

Children's Press®
A Division of Scholastic Inc.
New York / Toronto / London / Auckland / Sydney
Mexico City / New Delhi / Hong Kong
Danbury, Connecticut

Book Design: Michael DeLisio
Contributing Editor: Matthew Pitt
Photo Credits: All photos by Maura B. McConnell except pp. 5, 7, 17, 33,
42–48 © Artville

Library of Congress Cataloging-in-Publication Data

Fine, Jil.
Baby-sitting smarts / by Jil Fine.
   p. cm. – (Smarts)
Summary: Provides tips for teens on learning and practicing good
baby-sitting skills, getting baby-sitting jobs, preparing for a particular
job, handling emergencies, and duties after the children are asleep.
Includes bibliographical references and index.
ISBN 0-516-23926-0 (lib. bdg.) – ISBN 0-516-24011-0 (pbk.)
1. Babysitting–Handbooks, manuals, etc.–Juvenile literature. [1.
Babysitting–Handbooks, manuals, etc.] I. Title. II. Series.
HQ769.5 .F5 2002
649'.1'0248–dc21
                              2002002073

Contents

Help Wanted:

Responsible teen who wants to make money while having fun! Good money. Call Sally at (555) 555-5555

Want to earn a little extra cash? Are you good with kids? If you answered yes to both of these questions, baby-sitting might be the perfect job for you! Baby-sitting is a lot of fun, but it also requires a lot of knowledge and responsibility. The most important thing to know is how to keep the child you're caring for safe. This book will teach you basic first aid and important safety tips. This book will also prepare you for the world of baby-sitting. Everything from getting the job to tucking the kids in at night is discussed. If you follow the tips and instructions in the pages that follow, you'll be on your way to becoming a great baby-sitter in no time.

For busy parents, a responsible baby-sitter who is available for work is headline news.

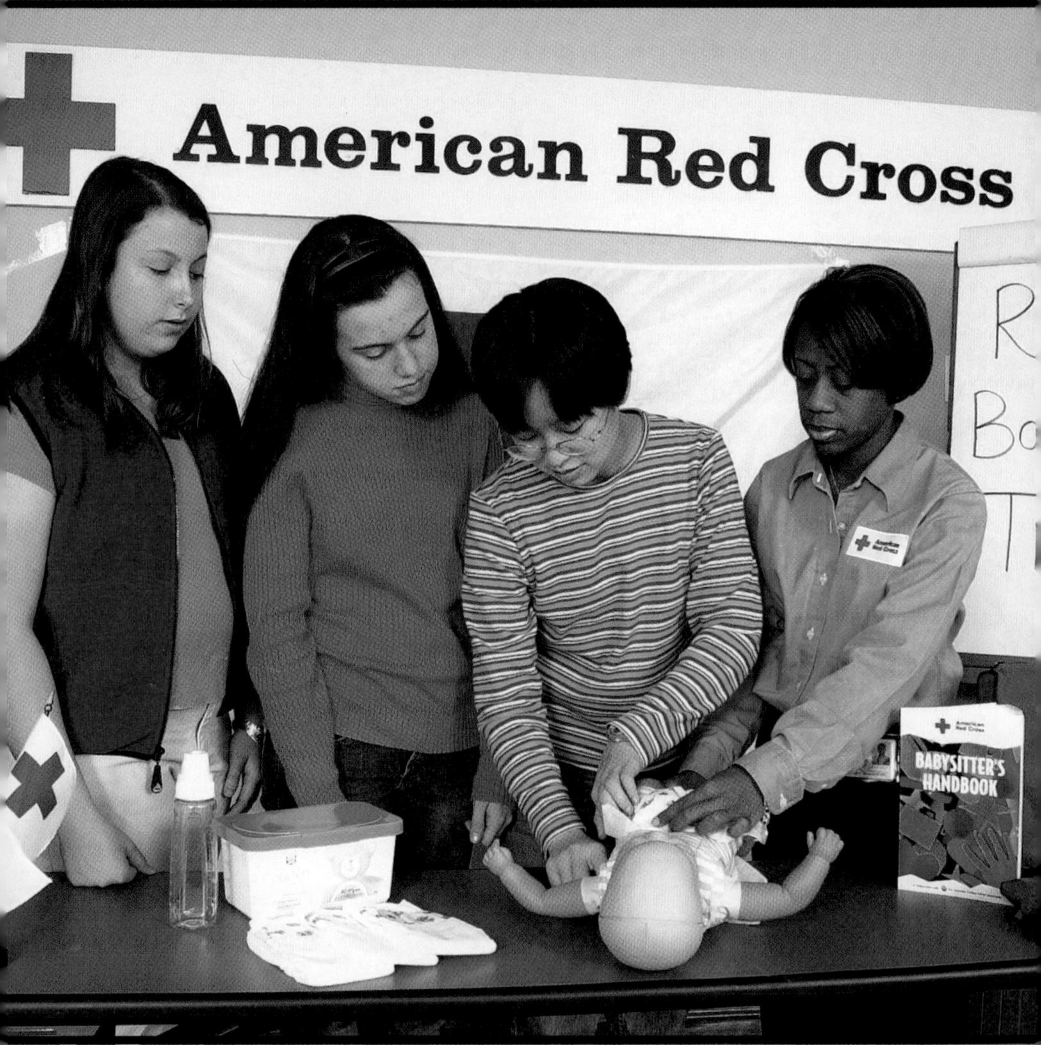
American Red Cross
American Red Cross
BABYSITTER'S HANDBOOK

Chapter 1

Jump into Sitting

There are many ways to get ready for your first baby-sitting job. One popular way to prepare is by taking a Red Cross baby-sitting class. Most local Red Cross agencies offer affordable baby-sitting classes for eleven to fifteen-year-olds. The Red Cross class teaches new baby-sitters important safety tips and life-saving skills. This class is highly respected and a great way to learn.

If you do take this class, let your potential clients know. If they're considering more than one person for the job, your extra knowledge may tip the odds in your favor!

If you cannot take a class with the Red Cross, try a different path. It helps to speak with family members or friends of your parents who have children.

Taking a Red Cross class is one of the best ways to improve your baby-sitting skills.

Ask if you can help them take care of their child while they're around. Use the time to ask them questions. You will be learning from people who know what it takes to care for a child. This will help both you and the parents. You'll gain some valuable knowledge, and they'll have an eager, extra pair of hands helping them out.

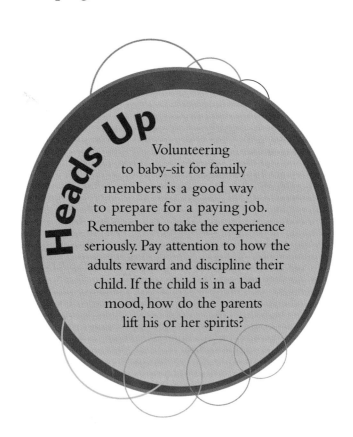

Heads Up

Volunteering to baby-sit for family members is a good way to prepare for a paying job. Remember to take the experience seriously. Pay attention to how the adults reward and discipline their child. If the child is in a bad mood, how do the parents lift his or her spirits?

Get Serious About Fun

Preparing to baby-sit also involves dreaming up fun ways to entertain children. Many baby-sitters bring along a bag of fun things to play with. The items you bring don't have to be expensive. Odds and ends that are lying around your house will do nicely. After all, they'll all be new to the child! Let your imagination roam—but keep the age of the child you're caring for in mind. Don't bring small things that a toddler or baby can swallow or choke on. Also, it's not wise to bring markers or pens with ink that can stain. Kids can be messy!

Heads Up

Here are some ideas of what to put in your bag:

- crayons
- paper lunch bags for coloring on or making into puppets
- glue
- big sidewalk chalk
- paper plates
- cheap construction paper
- old magazines, greeting cards, and scrap paper
- safety scissors
- nontoxic watercolors or fingerpaints
- an old shirt to use as a smock

Sally Chang

Baby-sitter Services
Caring and responsible.
I love children.
Rate: $5/per hour
$1 more for each
additional child
(555) 555-5555

Chapter 2

Getting the Job

Once you're prepared to baby-sit, you need to test your new skills. Baby-sitting is a business. The best and safest way to advertise in this business is by word-of-mouth. Talk to parents of young children in your community, school, or place of worship. Let them know that you are available to baby-sit. You may also want to make business cards to hand out to potential employers. Be sure to put your name and phone number on the cards. It's also a good idea to write down the rate that you plan to charge per hour. Never give your cards to strangers. Even though you may be anxious to start your new business, keep this rule in mind: You should only baby-sit for people you know.

Handing out your business cards to neighbors is a great way to get the word out: You're the right person for the job!

Sitting Pretty

Soon, the word will be out that a good baby-sitter is looking for work. When parents call, be prepared to discuss the rate that you will charge. A general rate is between three and seven dollars an hour. Sometimes, baby-sitters charge fifty cents to one dollar more an hour for each additional child. Baby-sitters may also charge more for an infant, since they need more attention and care. Before setting your rate, discuss the issue with your parents, along with any of your friends who baby-sit. This will help you figure out what the going rate is in your neighborhood.

Another issue to bring up when talking to your new employer is your schedule. Let him or her know when you are available and, if you have a curfew, at what time you must be home. Before agreeing to baby-sit, arrange your transportation to and from the job. Always have someone take you home at night. Never walk home alone.

Also, let your parents or guardians know about your baby-sitting plans. Be sure to tell them which

Some parents find it comforting to meet potential baby-sitters before offering them a job.

hours you are going to be working. Also provide them with the name, address, and phone number of the family you will be baby-sitting for.

Ask Away

Making a good first impression with a family is important. Call the family before the day of your

Heads Up

If your employers don't mind you having a snack, be sure not to chow down a five-course meal. They won't be happy if they return home to find an empty refrigerator.

job to ask some questions. (Be sure that they've got a minute to speak with you!) Take notes on each family that you baby-sit for. Many baby-sitters keep a file on each family, and then bring that file with them to each job. Creating a baby-sitting notebook will help keep all your information handy and organized.

Asking appropriate questions will make your baby-sitting experience safer and less worrisome. Doing this will show the parents that you are responsible. It will also let them know that you are truly concerned for their child's welfare. Before calling, write down the questions that you plan to ask. This way, you'll be sure not to forget anything important. If you get stuck trying to think of good questions, start with the following suggestions.

- Questions About Kids: Does the child have any special needs? Is he or she taking any medicine? If so, will you be responsible for giving it to the child? When and how much should you give?
- House Rules: How would the parents like you to deal with misbehavior? Are there any areas of the house where the child is forbidden to go? When is bedtime? Ask about rules concerning the use of the computer, the television, and the phone.
- A List of Duties: Do the parents expect you to take care of anything before they return? For instance, do you have to give the child a bath? Do they expect you to fix a meal for the child? If so, what does the child eat, and is there any food the child is allergic to? Are you expected to help the child with schoolwork? While on duty, are there house pets you will also need to care for?

Each family has its own routine. Asking questions ahead of time will help you understand just what that routine is—making it easier for you to follow.

Chapter 3

On the Job

The first time you baby-sit for a family, arrive a little early. Ask the parents to give you a brief tour of the house. As you stroll through each room, look around for possible safety hazards. Make sure that anything dangerous—like medicine, cleaning solutions, or alcohol—is stored in a locked cabinet. If the child is very young, look to see that stairways are gated and bathroom doors are shut. Swimming pools should also be gated or covered. Large objects that can fall or tip over need to remain out of a child's reach. Sharp objects should also be put away. If you see something unsafe, tell the parents. Think of possible fire exits and ask the parents if they have a family fire plan. Find out where emergency supplies, such as the first aid kit, flashlights, candles, and matches are kept.

Having baby-sitting smarts will help you turn a hazardous area into a safe one.

Number Crunching

Make sure to get emergency phone numbers. These important numbers should include the phone number of where the parents will be. If they have a cell phone or beeper, take down that number, too. You should also get the address and phone number of one of the family's neighbors. This could come in handy if the parents can't be reached. Also, be sure that you have numbers for the family doctor, the police and fire departments, and the poison control center. You should write down the address and phone number of where you are baby-sitting. If you need to call 911, it is important that you can tell the operator where you are. Keep all of this information near the phone. In the event of an emergency, you don't want to waste any precious moments.

Home Alone

You've gone through your safety check with the parents. Confidently, they say good-bye, leaving you in charge. Now you're ready for a fun evening with

Try to take a tour of unfamiliar homes. Have the parents point out any hazards or safety features, such as the latch on this cabinet door.

your young companion. Hold on—not so fast! Your little friend is screaming, upset to see her parents leave. What do you do? First, tell her that you are only going to be there for a little while. Then, assure her that you two are going to have some fun. Tell the child that her parents will be home that night. She will see them then, or first thing in the morning. Try to distract the child: Play with a toy or make funny faces. Your greatest ally is your imagination. Anything that makes the child laugh will get your evening off to a fine start.

Heads Up

Keep those house doors locked! Don't let a stranger in, and don't let anyone know that you are the baby-sitter. If you think someone suspicious is lurking outside, don't investigate. Call the police. It's better to have an officer check it out than to take the risk yourself.

Safety First

Children are extremely curious. Sometimes they do seemingly fun things that are actually harmful.

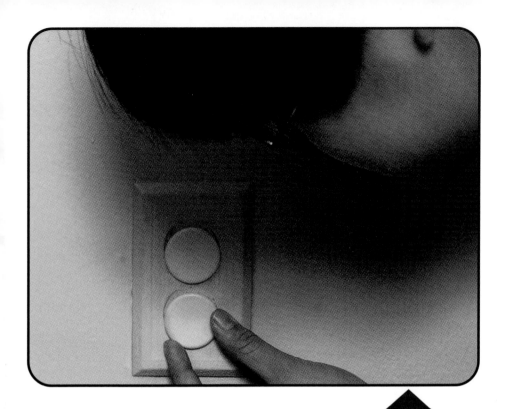

Kids tend to touch before thinking, which is why this baby-sitter is making sure the electric outlets are covered up.

No matter how hard you prepare and work to keep them safe, kids may still find a way to get into harm's way. Knowing some basic first aid steps can really help you out.

Let's say the child cuts his knee. The first thing you should do is wash your hands. After your hands are clean, wash the cut with mild soap or water. If the family has antibacterial ointment, put some on the cut.

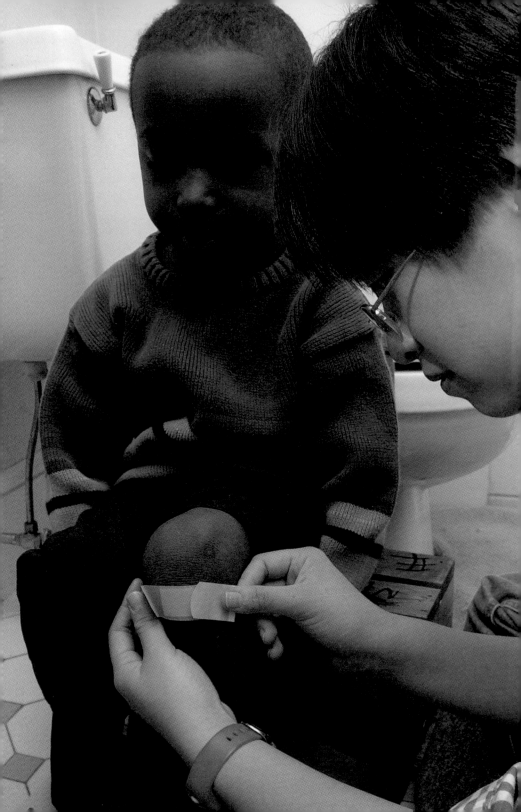

Then, apply a clean bandage. If the cut is deep and looks bad, make sure to wash your hands, but do not wash the wound. Washing a bad wound can make it bleed more. Instead, apply pressure just above the wound to slow the bleeding. Once the situation is under control—or if you can't get it under control—call 911. If there is an object in the wound, don't try to remove it. Let an Emergency Medical Technician (EMT) or doctor examine it. After calling 911, follow up with a phone call to the parents. Following these tips will lower the risk of infection and serious injury.

Fun for All Ages

Fun is an important part of baby-sitting. One way to make baby-sitting fun is by creating engaging activities for you and the child to do together. In addition to the items in your baby-sitting bag, you should know what kids of different ages can (and like to) do. Knowing the child's interests will make the evening a fun, relaxed, and safe one.

Tending to minor scrapes and cuts is part of a baby-sitter's job. But you should leave really serious injuries to the professionals.

Many kids love to show their creative sides to their sitters.

Infants

Babies like to be held, sung to, and rocked. They like to play with brightly colored toys and things that make noise, such as rattles. Babies are excited by the world around them and love to see new, colorful things. Take care to make sure that what they play with is clean, soft, and safe. Toys should not fit into a baby's mouth.

CPR Basics

CPR stands for Cardiopulmonary Resuscitation. CPR is a way to keep someone breathing when that person becomes unconscious, or passes out. If a child between the ages of one and eight passes out, follow these steps:

1. Check for any response or breathing. Check the child's pulse by placing your first two fingers under the child's ear, near the jawbone.
2. Tilt the child's head back and listen for breathing. Grunting, gasping, or snoring are signs of struggle and should not be considered normal breathing. If the child isn't breathing normally, pinch his or her nose and cover his or her mouth with yours. Blow until the child's chest rises. Give two breaths.
3. Listen for breathing. If the child doesn't start breathing on his or her own, press the heel of your hand on the child's sternum. The sternum is located between the nipples on the chest. Push down with the heel of your hand about 1 to 1 ½ inches. Push down five times. A good way to time your pushes is to count, "One and two and three and four and five."
4. Check for any signs of breathing. If there are none, give the child another breath.
5. Repeat steps three and four for one minute. Then, quickly but calmly, dial 911. Continue to perform CPR until help arrives.

Note: The instructions above should be followed only as a guideline. To receive proper training, be sure to complete a CPR course.

While it may be easy to entertain babies, they require lots of attention. You should always be alert when baby-sitting an infant. *Never* leave a baby unattended.

Older Children

Drawing is fun for kids of all ages. The best things for toddlers to use for drawing are fat, unwrapped crayons. Toddlers' hands are still very small, and big crayons are easier for them to hold. Try to tape down the paper that they are drawing on so that it doesn't move around. Older children like to draw, too. Another fun activity to try is writing a short story, then having the child draw pictures to match it. Or, create puppets from lunch bags and put on a play. With a little imagination, crayons and paper can provide hours of amusement.

Making music is another way to bring some joy and flair to the evening. Empty butter tubs or oat-meal boxes make great drums. You and the child can dance and sing, composing your own words. There are plenty of ways to have fun while baby-sitting.

If the child you're sitting for likes music, you can turn a few pots and pans into a smashing success!

Keep your eyes open for new ideas. From board games to reading to homework—keep the child amused, and the hours will fly by for the both of you!

End of the Night

You've had a great evening, and bedtime is approaching. If you were asked to give the child a bath, make sure you watch her the entire time. It only takes a few inches of water for a child to drown. The water should be warm, but not hot. A good way to test the water is by dipping your elbow in. If you are bathing a baby, always keep one hand on her so that she doesn't slip.

Sometimes, even for an experienced sitter, getting kids to go to bed is a monumental task. There are things you can do to save time and tears. Ten minutes before bedtime, give the child a warning. This lets him know what to expect and prepares him for it.

Many kids need to calm down before bedtime. Reading books or listening to soft music can help. Give your child a choice as to which activity she

Reading a child's favorite book at night helps calm him or her down before bedtime.

would like to do before bed. Say something like, "Would you like to read 'Little Red Riding Hood' or 'The Ugly Duckling' tonight?" This way, the child feels like she has some say in what's happening.

Once the child has fallen asleep, you should quietly check on her or him every 15 minutes or so.

Use the time before the parents get home to clean up any mess you made. Do the dishes and put away any stray toys. Try to leave things exactly as they were when you arrived.

When the parents return, give them a brief rundown of the evening. Let them know if their child got hurt, broke anything, or if anything else out of the ordinary happened. Figure out how many hours you worked and how much you are owed. If the parents appear to have been drinking and you are supposed to get a ride home from them, do not accept. Instead, call your parents or a neighbor to pick you up. Don't be afraid to stop baby-sitting for a family if you feel uncomfortable around the parents or don't get along with the child. There are plenty of families looking for a good sitter. You should not stay in a situation that makes you uncomfortable.

Just because the child is sleeping doesn't mean the baby-sitter's work is done. Always check in on the child after bedtime to make sure all is well.

Be sure that the parents you're working for are willing and able to take you back home.

Chapter 4

Are You Experienced?

The following story describes the first job of a baby-sitter named Sally. As you read, think about Sally's choices. Are they all good decisions? Think about what you might do differently if you were in the same situation.

Sally's Sitting Experience

Sally arrived at Mr. and Mrs. Marshall's house at 5:45 P.M. to baby-sit for their two-year-old son, Jack. Mrs. Marshall wrote down her cell phone number on a slip of paper, then handed it to Sally. Sally put the number into her pocket and went over to play with Jack. As the parents were leaving,

> Providing the child with a few fun activities can help make your sitting experience go much more smoothly.

they asked Sally if she had any questions. Sally shook her head no and continued playing.

After a few minutes, Jack didn't want to play anymore and started to get upset. Sally remembered that she had brought along markers and a coloring book. She and Jack went into the kitchen and sat at the table. Jack scribbled all over the pages of the coloring books. Soon, his artwork was also all over the table. When Sally tried to take the markers away, Jack even drew on her new shirt.

Now, Jack was screaming and crying. Sally took him into the living room. She picked up one of Jack's stuffed animals and started making funny animal noises. After a few minutes, Jack was smiling again.

Jack had calmed down, but his cheeks were still red. Sally felt his forehead and face. He felt very warm. Sally decided to take his temperature. She looked in the bathroom for a thermometer, but couldn't find it. After a few minutes of frantic searching, Sally found the thermometer in the kitchen. When Sally returned to the living room. Jack was lying on the sofa, playing with a toy.

Some children are better than others at reporting when they feel ill. If you have a hunch that the child you're sitting for is sick, follow it up.

Sally took Jack's temperature. It was 100 degrees Farenheit (38 degrees Celsius). Sally decided to call Jack's parents and let them know that their son was running a fever. However, the piece of paper with the Marshalls' cell phone number wasn't in her pocket!

She looked everywhere, but couldn't find it. Sally called her mom. Sally's mom told her to give Jack some water. Since the two families were friends with each other, Sally was able to get the Marshalls' cell phone number. As soon as Sally hung up the phone, she gave Jack a glass of water. Then, she called the Marshalls. They told her that they were in the middle of dinner and would come home as soon as possible.

Sally helped Jack into pajamas and had him choose a book to read before bed. Soon, Jack was asleep. After trying, and failing, to wash the stains out of her shirt, Sally went into the kitchen. She worked hard to clean the marker stains from the table. By the time the Marshalls got home, Sally had cleaned most of the stains off. Mr. Marshall paid Sally and drove her home.

Another Look at Sally

Sally did many things right, but she also could have made some better choices. What would you have

It's important to keep contact information, such as telephone numbers, in one place. That way, you won't have to scramble in an emergency.

done differently? Let's consider her decisions from the beginning.

To start, Sally should have written down the parents' cell phone number, along with other important numbers, and left them by the phone. Luckily, her mom was home and was able to help her out.

It was great that Sally brought along activities to share with Jack. She shouldn't have brought markers, though. Those are too difficult, and messy, for a two-year-old to play with. Sally learned the hard way that markers stain clothes. Crayons would have been a better choice.

Sally made the right decision to take Jack into the living room when he started misbehaving. She knew to take him away from what was making him upset. Making him laugh with the stuffed animal was also a good move. Sally was able to take control of the situation and keep Jack from getting more upset.

When Sally saw that Jack looked feverish, she did well in acting quickly—maybe too quickly. A baby-sitter should never leave a child alone, especially a child as young as Jack. Sally was lucky that

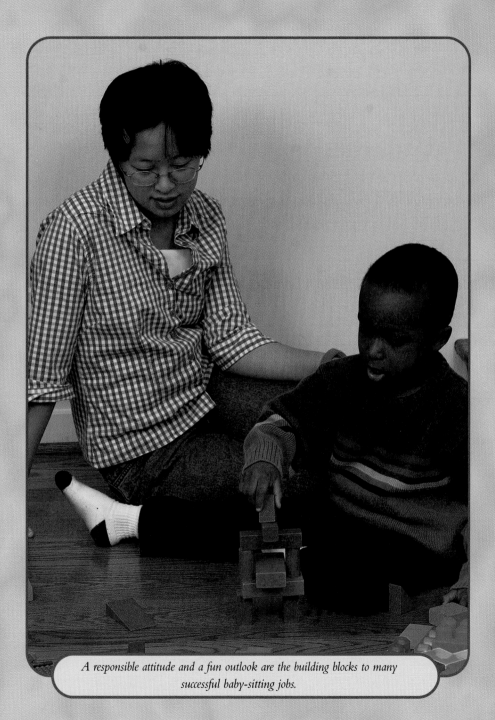

A responsible attitude and a fun outlook are the building blocks to many successful baby-sitting jobs.

Jack didn't wander off or get hurt. She could have avoided her long search for the thermometer if she had asked the Marshalls where their first aid supplies were kept before they left.

When Sally read the thermometer and saw that Jack did have a low fever, she did the right thing by calling her mother. She acted quickly to help Jack by notifying his parents. Most of the time, a fever is not a big enough emergency to call 911. However, a high fever can be very dangerous. It's important to let the parents know as soon as possible that their child is ill.

Sally did a good job managing bedtime and getting Jack to sleep. She also proved how responsible she was when she cleaned the table before the Marshalls returned. Sally made mistakes but, in general, was a good sitter. She acted quickly and calmly when things went wrong. If you learn from Sally's mistakes and follow her good examples, you'll be on your way to becoming a prepared, responsible—and well-paid—baby-sitter.

> *Don't forget: You're not alone. In an emergency, you have firefighters, doctors, and police officers all within your reach. They're just a few digits away.*

allergic a physical reaction to things like pollen, food, or plants

antibacterial something that kills bacteria, which is a microscopic living thing that may cause disease

Cardiopulmonary Resuscitation (CPR) a method of reviving someone using mouth-to-mouth breathing and chest compressions

curfew a rule that dictates a specific time when you have to be home

entertain to amuse and interest someone

hazards dangers or risks

life-saving done to save someone's life

ointment a thick, often greasy substance put on the skin to heal or protect it

rate a charge or fee

responsible to be trusted and have important duties

suspicious a concern that something is wrong or bad

thermometer an instrument used to measure temperature

transportation a means of getting from place to place

word-of-mouth to speak about someone's talents or character; to give a reference

American Red Cross Staff. *American Red Cross Baby-sitter's Handbook.* St. Louis, MO: Mosby–Year Book, Incorporated, 1998.

Brown, Harriet N. *The Babysitter's Handbook.* Middleton, WI: Pleasant Company Publications, 1999.

Kuck, K.D. *The Babysitter's Handbook.* New York, NY: Random House Books for Young Readers, 1997.

Vavolizza, Christine and Mark. *Every Baby-sitter Needs This Book.* White Plains, NY: Peter Pauper Press, Incorporated, 1998.

Zakarin, Debra Mostow. *The Ultimate Baby-Sitter's Handbook.* New York, NY: Putnam Publishing Group, 1997.

Organizations

American Red Cross Headquarters

Attn: Public Inquiry Office
1621 North Kent Street, 11th Floor
Arlington, VA 22209
(703) 248-4222

Safe Sitter

5670 Caito Drive, Suite 172
Indianapolis, IN 46226
(317) 355-4888

Web Sites

American Red Cross—Babysitter's Training Course

www.redcross.org/services/hss/courses/babyindex.html
Find out about the baby-sitter's training
course on this Web site. You can also learn
some important baby-sitting tips and find
your local Red Cross chapter.

CBC4Kids Baby-sitting Guide
http://www.cbc4kids.ca/general/kids-club/babysitters/ started.html
This Web site has a detailed baby-sitting guide. It includes tips on getting started, fun activities to do on the job, and other important information.

The Nemours Foundation: TeensHealth—Baby-sitting Basics
http://kidshealth.org/teen/mind_matters/school/ babysit.html
Learn lots of important information about baby-sitting on this informative Web site.

Index

Index

About the Author
Jil Fine spent many a night baby-sitting her younger brother—and he turned out just fine.